Wedding Favors

Wedding Favors

Antonia Swinson

RYLAND
PETERS
& SMALL

LONDON NEW YORK

First published in the United States in 2006 by
Ryland Peters & Small, Inc
519 Broadway, 5th Floor
New York, NY 10012
www.rylandpeters.com

10 9 8 7 6 5 4 3 2 1
Text, design, and photographs
© Ryland Peters & Small 2006

Library of Congress Cataloging-in-Publication
Data

Swinson, Antonia.
  Wedding favors fabulous favors for the perfect
wedding day / by Antonia Swinson.
    p. cm.
  ISBN-13: 978-1-84597-106-9
  ISBN-10: 1-84597-106-X
  1. Wedding decorations. 2. Handicraft. 3. Table
setting and decoration. I. Title.
  TT900.P3S95 2006
  747'.93--dc22
                            2005022042

Printed in China

Senior Designer Sonya Nathoo

Editor Martha Keenan

Commissioning Editor Annabel Morgan

Picture Researcher Emily Westlake

Production Gemma Moules

Art Director Anne-Marie Bulat

Editorial Director Julia Charles

Publishing Director Alison Starling

contents

introduction

Everyone loves being given a present. Handing out mementoes, or favors, to wedding guests is a time-honored tradition, a small but significant way in which the bride and groom can say thank you to friends and family for their generosity, support, and good wishes.

As with any gift, the thought is more important than the contents, and for those on a budget, there are dozens of ideas here for favors that are every bit as cost-effective as they are appealing. There are delicious edible goodies, such as cookies, cakes, chocolates, and candies (many of which can be made at home), as well as flowers, candles, and scented gifts; and luxurious keepsakes for special members of the wedding party. There are also ideas galore for beautiful packaging and fabulous presentation.

Whatever your taste, creative abilities, and budget, you're sure to find something that both you and your guests will love!

fabulous favors

What will you delight your wedding guests with? Whatever your taste and budget, there are favors to suit: delectable cakes, cookies, chocolates, and candies; dainty napkins and handkerchiefs; romantic flowers; scented delights; magical candles; beautiful bags; and special keepsakes.

edible goodies

COOKIES

Cookies are an inexpensive but universally popular choice of wedding favor. Whether homemade or purchased, you can choose from cookies that are buttery and plain, macaroon-crumbly, perfumed with vanilla or lemon, or studded with chocolate chips or nuts. For a fall or winter wedding, cookies laced with sweet aromatic spices such as cinnamon, ginger, or cloves—or, more extravagantly, gleaming with real gold leaf—would evoke the season perfectly.

Shaped cookies always look appealing. Cutters can be bought in every conceivable shape and size from kitchen retailers and mail-order suppliers. Hearts are an obvious and undeniably romantic choice, or you could opt for stars, flowers, butterflies, birds, or your initials. If you want to decorate your cookies, try color-coordinating them with the flowers or wedding dress for a professional look. A simple, smooth coating of royal icing looks

Distributing favors to friends and family is a symbolic gesture with ancient roots, a recognition of the guests' role in supporting and witnessing the marriage.

effective and can be further embellished with gold or silver balls, sugar flowers, or sparkling colored sugars and powders, which are available from cake-decorating suppliers.

If you're an experienced home cook or are having your cookies professionally made, they could be iced with intricate patterns or a motif that has a special meaning for you. They could even be shaped and decorated to look like miniature wedding cakes. Cookies could also be iced with initials or names, whether they be yours or those of your guests. If cookies are iced with guests' names, they can double up as place markers, as shown on page 13. Here, rectangular cookies imitate name tags, iced in delicious pastel shades and finished with matching ribbon (just remember to pierce the hole before baking).

Fine ribbon can also be used to hang cookies up for display, perhaps from branches arranged in a vase or, in winter, from Christmas trees and ivy wreaths. Cookies also look good packaged in boxes (see opposite, above right), nestling in pretty paper-lined baskets (below left), or laid out neatly on a platter of rose petals.

CUPCAKES

During a ceremony called *confarreatio,* the most binding form of marriage in ancient Rome, the bridal couple shared a sweet cake. Presenting your guests with cake favors echoes this and many other centuries-old wedding traditions. Like cookies, cakes can easily be produced at home and are a versatile vehicle for decoration.

Cupcakes have simple charm and can be topped with icing and other goodies, such as chocolate curls, sugar flowers, gold or silver balls, crystallized fresh flowers, candy, fresh fruit, or gold leaf. They can also be

iced with names or initials. Even simple purchased cakes, such as the pastel-colored petits fours shown on the left, look tempting when presented with flair.

Another approach is to give each guest a miniature wedding cake, iced to resemble its full-scale parent. For a December wedding, tiny Christmas fruitcakes might be fun. Other sweet mouthfuls to consider include tiny scones and miniature tarts or chocolate tortes.

CHOCOLATES

When it comes to luxury, few things beat luscious, indulgent chocolate. Prettily packaged (here, in a box printed with antique engravings, lined with tissue and tied with ribbon), they'll be irresistible to your guests.

If your budget allows, you could splash out on handmade chocolates such as palest pink white-chocolate truffles (see page 21), sumptuous continental-style chocolates, or old-fashioned rose or violet creams. A professional chocolatier may be able to personalize your chocolates with a motif, name, or initials, using dark chocolate against white, or vice versa, for a striking contrast.

If money's more of an issue, chocolate truffles are easy to produce at home from chocolate, cream, and various flavorings (such as vanilla or liqueur), and your guests will undoubtedly appreciate the effort you've put into them. If you're making your own, it's worth using really good-quality chocolate with a 70 percent cocoa solids content. Homemade truffles can be rolled in cocoa powder or chopped nuts (try almonds or pistachios), or dipped in melted chocolate (see page 20).

Wrapped chocolates are another option. Here (left), golden hearts have been placed in a wineglass to double as place markers, complete with coordinating gold name tags. For variations on the chocolate theme, consider chocolate-covered coffee beans to be served with the coffee, chocolate-dipped miniature meringues, or chocolate-dipped fruit. For a spring wedding, offer chocolate eggs in little baskets lined with moss and primroses.

Chocolates of all kinds look elegant in petit-four cases, tucked inside paper cones, or placed in cellophane bags tied with fancy ribbon. If you're going to bring them out at the end of the meal, you could wrap them in twists of brightly colored tissue paper and pile them into coffee cups (see page 58).

CANDY

For favors with a bit of fun and frivolity, candies are a great choice. Jordan almonds are one of the most popular favors, and have a long association with weddings (the Romans threw sweet almonds over newlywed couples, a practice which developed into throwing confetti). Almonds have for centuries been associated with fertility and abundance, and it's traditional to give guests five to represent health, wealth, happiness,

fertility, and long life. Jordan almonds are a versatile choice, too, because they're available in a huge choice of colors, so can coordinate with any scheme. They look wonderful heaped into dishes such as the one shown on the left, which doubles as a table number, or bundled up in small circles of paper or tulle fabric.

Jelly beans also come in lots of tempting colors and flavors, though for a more sophisticated approach you might like to stick to just one

(above right, white beans look elegant in cellophane cones finished with mint-green ribbon). Just as chic are the white mints shown here in cellophane bundles. Pastel gummy bears, jelly babies, stick candy, candy love hearts, or fruity lollipops will no doubt encourage your guests to revisit their childhoods and should provoke a smile or two. Present candy in bags or boxes, or fill baskets with them and invite your guests to pick and mix. You could even sprinkle your tables with edible confetti.

floral favors

POSIES AND POTS

If scent, color, and beauty are qualities you admire, look no farther than flowers for your favors. For centuries, they've been an intrinsic part of weddings, representing love, beauty, and fertility. You could present guests with posies in tiny silver pots, as shown here, glasses or small vases (see page 27), paper cones, rustic baskets, vintage perfume bottles, or pretty coffee cups. Even humble jelly jars can be dressed up with a sash of ribbon and filled with unpretentious country garden-style flowers.

Roses are a traditional choice, but also a practical one, because they last well and come in countless colors. Other flowers that will look good all day are carnations, tulips, gerberas, and lilies. If scent is important, consider using sweet peas, garden roses, old-fashioned pinks, stocks, or lavender. Scented spring delights include narcissi and hyacinths. The alternative to cut flowers is to fill pots with plants that guests can continue to enjoy at home. Even during the depths of winter, bulbs such as narcissi and hyacinths can be "forced" into blooming (ask at your local garden center for advice). In spring you could try lily of the valley or violas; in summer, there are scented exotics such as jasmine or stephanotis.

The tradition of the
bridal bouquet goes back
centuries. It originally
consisted of herbs, which
were thought to have
the power to ward off
evil spirits.

PERFECT BLOOMS

A single exquisite flower is beautiful enough to be a favor in its own right.
If you're going to use fresh blooms (see below left), they must be perfect
examples, with long, straight stems. They can be decorated with ribbon, to
which you could attach a message for your guests or suitable lines of
poetry. Roses are a classic choice (strip thorns from the stems before
use), and they last well when cut. Others to try include tulips, carnations,
lilies, camellias, gardenias, gerberas, and hydrangeas (useful for late summer
and autumn color), or, in winter, amaryllis.

Fabric flowers (from craft and department stores, interiors stores, and

garden centers) are a good alternative to fresh ones,
having the advantage of being permanent
mementoes. You'll also be able to source flowers in
any color, shape, and size, regardless of the season.
The gorgeous blowsy, variegated roses shown
opposite, complete with leaves and buds, look every
bit as good as the real thing.

non-edible keepsakes

HANDKERCHIEFS AND NAPKINS

It might seem a little mundane to offer your guests handkerchiefs or napkins as favors. However, if they are stylishly presented, they make highly decorative permanent keepsakes.

Large linen double damask napkins are considered to be the finest quality. For favors, however, you might want something rather smaller in a finer, less expensive fabric, or pretty cotton handkerchiefs. White is the traditional choice for table linen, although dreamy pastels such as candy pink, baby blue, and mint green could look very romantic. For a fall celebration, slubbed silk in rich golds and warm oranges would echo the season's colors perfectly.

Pretty details—fancy edging, delicate embroidery, and lace—will help to lift napkins and handkerchiefs out of the ordinary, while embroidered monograms or initials will add a pleasingly personal touch.

You might want to put a favor—such as wrapped chocolates, candy, or scented soap—inside your napkins. Alternatively, you could secure napkins with decorative rings as an extra present. These could be bought for the purpose; otherwise, you could use ribbon, braid, or cord, adding anything else that takes your fancy, such as beads, feathers, shells, or mother-of-pearl buttons. You could also experiment with different ways of folding your napkins—try rolling them, cinching them in the middle, or folding them into a square, tying them at one end and fanning them out.

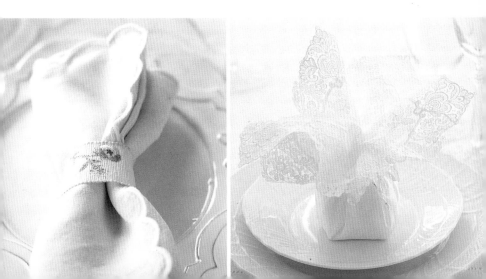

SCENTED GIFTS

Favors that are beautifully scented will always be well received, particularly by female guests. Sachets or bags made from fine cotton or linen can be bought or run up at home, and are ideal for filling with dried lavender, rose petals, or pot pourri. These can then be used to scent drawers or placed under pillows (you could pin instructions to your favors). Bags or paper envelopes are ideal for small bars of fragrant soap, soap leaves, bath bombs, or bath salts (anything loose must be contained in a plastic inner bag to prevent spillage). You could also give guests incense cones or miniatures of room scent, bath foam, body lotion, or other toiletries.

CANDLES

Associated as they are with purity, hope, and truth, candles make romantic and symbolic favors. Those made from beeswax (see far left) are the slowest burning and have a natural, rustic appeal, although they are more expensive than standard, paraffin-based candles.

Long, slender candles are easy to package. Bundle a few together and wrap them in paper or fabric before tying with a length of ribbon or cord. Chunky pillar candles can be decorated with a sash of wide ribbon, silk, or lace. Fine tapers look slender and elegant secured with satin cord and presented on a silver platter (see left). Tealights are great value and could be presented in clear or colored glass votive holders.

Other possibilities include scented candles, floating candles, and those molded into attractive shapes such as flowers, hearts, or fruits.

FABRIC BAGS

Decorative bags are special enough to be gifts in themselves. You could either buy them or make them at home—this sort of project needs little sewing experience. Look in fabric stores for fine linen, silk, taffeta, or velvet.

If you're giving your bridesmaids special little bags on the wedding day, why not fill them with confetti for throwing after the ceremony? For the most romantic effect, choose dried flower petals, such as roses, delphiniums, or aromatic lavender.

Bags can be trimmed with braid, feathers, ribbon, or lace, and detailed with sequins and beads or, to enhance the personal nature of the gift, an embroidered monogram. For a fastening, choose from a cord drawstring neck, ribbon ties, or an unusual decorative button.

SPECIAL GIFTS

If you're having an intimate wedding with just a handful of guests, you may want to go to town on your favors and splash out on more permanent keepsakes. Very special mementoes are also appropriate for key members of the bridal party—the parents, attendants, and best man.

Any mall will have gift shops, department stores, and jewelers brimming with suitable items. However, if you're after something really unusual,

browse around antique or secondhand stores, or your local consignment house. You may be surprised how inexpensively you can pick up small vintage and antique items such as the silver-lidded salt and pepper pots, and mother-of-pearl demitasse spoons shown opposite.

Look out for silver teaspoons, too, or pill boxes, picture frames, old perfume bottles, cufflinks, letter openers, teacups and saucers, or candle holders. Place-card holders such as the charming porcelain bunny shown top right are another idea and can form part of the table setting. You could also buy silver napkin rings, or something like these delicate porcelain roses (centre right). More luxurious still are these silk tassels (right), finished in softest mink and designed originally to be used as key rings.

echo an accent color used in your flower arrangements. Gold and silver boxes (see pages 50 and 60) hint at luxurious contents, and printed boxes (see page 18) have quirky charm.

Lining your boxes with tissue paper or a doily will add to your guests' pleasure in opening them. You've then got the fun of decorating the outside of your boxes. Ribbon always looks good, whether it's the same color as your boxes (see above right) or a contrasting one (see opposite). Narrow ribbon looks dainty, while wide ribbon tied into large bows gives packaging an extravagant flourish. Other decorative details can then be added, such as fresh

or fabric flowers (see pages 6 and 48), name tags (see page 48), beads, shells, or feathers.

Deciding how to present your favors is the final creative stage. You might want to use the boxes as part of your table setting, placing one on each plate (see below and opposite) or in each glass (see page 49). If you're placing them on your tables, you could add a name tag to each box. Another approach is to turn your boxes into centerpieces by arranging them on cake stands (see page 49), which can also display table

numbers. You could also lay the boxes out in perfect rows on a large table at the entrance to your reception so that guests can help themselves. If you decide to arrange them on large trays or platters, decorate these with strings of wired beads (see page 43), rose petals, or fresh flowers. On page 47, little sprigs of snowberries have been tucked in among the pristine white boxes to add a natural touch to the display.

WRAPPINGS AND RIBBONS

The tiniest token of appreciation is made all the more meaningful when it is thoughtfully presented. And wedding favors provide an ideal opportunity for you to have fun with pretty ribbons, paper, and trimmings.

Small envelopes are ideal receptacles for favors such as confetti, specially blended loose tea, or garden seeds (choose colorful annuals and include planting instructions). Secure the envelopes with sealing wax (stamped, perhaps, with a monogram) or tie them with a length of narrow ribbon. Pile them onto glass dishes or place them along lengths of wide ribbon that have been pinned to a tablecloth (see pages 54–55).

Paper cones can hold posies or Jordan almonds, and look good neatly stacked in wicker or metal baskets. Colored tissue paper can be twisted loosely around candies or chocolates. Using two contrasting colors looks particularly effective (see page 58). Bundles of favors can be made with sheer fabrics—organza, net, or tulle—or cellophane. Place these on guests' plates or in wineglasses, or display the favors en masse on platters, trays, or shallow baskets.

Small sachets, pouches, and bags are useful for loose items such as candy, flower seeds, or pot pourri. Waxed-paper bags tied with a piece of raffia or ribbon can hold anything from hard candy to birdseed confetti, to be distributed to guests (see page 52). To make your own bags, use a small book as a mold. Wrap paper around the book and tape the seam, then fold up and tape one end. Remove the book and crease the long sides to make a bag shape. Put your favor inside and fold the top down twice, gluing it or securing the bag with ribbon.

Favors are intended to provide guests with a happy reminder of the day, so you might want to give them an extract of poetry, a wise saying, or a message of thanks, handwritten on sheets of pretty paper. Roll these messages into scrolls, tie them with ribbon or cord, and display them in shallow dishes (see page 57), on trays, or in small galvanized buckets with a large note inviting guests to help themselves.

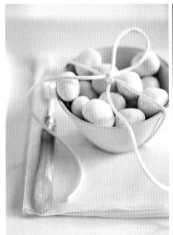

To wrap your favors, search stationery or craft stores for papers with interesting patterns, colors, and textures. Experiment with layering sheer tissue or tracing paper over colored paper, or using strips of paper woven in and out. Ribbon comes into its own here—simply tying wide ribbon into a large bow produces a glamorous look. Visit craft or stationery stores to find patterned, wired, or sheer ribbon, braid, cord, and other trimmings. Simple approaches are often the most chic (see the bowl of bonbons tied with white silk cord shown opposite). Layering various widths and textures of ribbon produces pretty effects, and you can add other embellishments such as fabric flowers, feathers, shells, or beads.

COLORS

It helps to give your reception a stylish look if all the details, including the favors, contribute to an overall color scheme. White is, of course, the classic wedding color, and an all-white theme (see pages 56–57) looks very chic.

But, if you want to introduce color, the easiest way is to pick a single accent, such as fresh blue (see the ribbon-tied box on page 49) or soft pink (see the paper-wrapped cake far left below). If you want to combine colors, pastels all work well together. A mixture of bright colors can look charming, but juxtapose with plenty of white so they don't clash or overwhelm the eye.

METALLICS

Gleaming shades of gold, silver, and bronze look grown-up and glamorous. For maximum interest, mix textures and finishes, and add beads, baubles, and ribbons.

For a December wedding, tie a tree ornament or a dreidel to your favors as an extra gift, reflecting the spirit of the season.

sources

BEAUCOUP
www.beau-coup.com
Wedding and bridal shower
favors, including candles,
sachets, soaps, silver
keepsakes, and custom-
designed cookies.

BELLATERRA
www.bellaterra.net
Packaging and invitation
design as well as well-priced
flower seeds, candy tins,
matches, and CD covers.

BEVERLY CLARK
Visit www.beverlyclark.com
for a retailer near you.
Cake boxes and other
presentation ideas.

CONFETTI
www.confetti-event.com
Boxes and custom-
monogrammed tags, plus
hand-dipped pretzel sticks
and pink French meringues.

CRABTREE & EVELYN
Visit www.crabtree-
evelyn.com for a retailer
near you.
Miniature soaps, bath gels,
and other toiletries.

GODIVA
Visit www.godiva.com for
a retailer near you.
Two- or four-chocolate
assortments in beribboned
gold ballotins.

JEAN M ESSENTIALS
Call 800-766-8595 or visit
www.jeanmessentials.com
to request a catalog.
Favour boxes, bags, and tins,
as well as tags, seals,
ribbons, and other
adornments. Also candles,
bubbles, and personalized
gifts.

KEEPSAKE FAVORS
www.keepsakefavors.com
Sweet treats, including
lollipops, Jordan almonds,
foil-wrapped chocolates and
heart-shaped candy in a
wide choice of colors.

MY OWN LABELS
www.myownlabels.com
Personalized labels and hang-tags, plus Chinese take-out boxes, tiny burlap bags, heart-shaped tins, and other presentation ideas.

PEARL RIVER
www.pearlriver.com
Colorful, stylish, and affordable Chinese imports, from paper decorations and lacquered chopsticks to quirky candles and satin pincushions.

ROLLING PIN PRODUCTIONS
www.rollingpinproductions.com
Monogrammed wedding-cake and heart-shaped cookie favors.

ROMANTIC FLOWERS
www.romanticflowers.com
Silk petals, flowers, and bouquets. Also wide range of favor boxes, ribbons, and other wrappings, including monogrammed stickers.

TOPS MALIBU
www.topsmalibu.com
Cupcake and fortune-cookie shaped candles, sparklers, pretty tags, butterfly confetti, and many more fun and unusual favors.

VOSGES HAUT-CHOCOLAT
520 North Michigan Avenue
Chicago, IL 60611
Call 888-301-9688 or visit www.vosgeschocolate.com for details of other stores or a retailer near you. *Chic chocolate treats, including the Sophie bars, which are ideal for bridal showers.*

WEDDING THINGS
www.weddingthings.com
Stylish keepsakes and packaging, including affordable monogrammed items.

YOUR WEDDING
www.yourweddingcompany.com
Lavender sachets, loose lavender, coffee and tea favors, and tree seeds.

picture credits

All photographs by Polly Wreford
apart from:

Sandra Lane

Pages 14 all, 20 center, 20 below,
36 left, 56 both, 60 left and 61 right

David Brittain

Page 27 right

perfect presentation

When displaying your favors, give your creativity free rein. Will you package them in neat little boxes topped with exuberant bows or pretty bags embellished with beads? Will you pile them on platters scattered with rose petals or lay them out in perfect rows on a pristine white tablecloth?

BOXES

Easy to decorate and present, boxes make fast work of packaging favors, particularly edibles such as cookies, chocolates, and candies.

Square boxes are neat and easy to stack, but you'll find other shapes at paper stores and wedding suppliers, including circular and heart-shaped ones; deep lidded boxes (see page 6); and shallow, rectangular ones (see page 60). Clear plastic boxes (see page 8) look good if you've got something particularly pretty to put inside, and it's also possible to buy small aluminum tins specially designed for holding favors.

White paper boxes like the ones shown opposite are a good blank canvas for decoration. Corrugated or embossed cardboard (see pages 51 and 58) adds textural interest, or you might choose a pastel tint to